OFFICIALLY NOTED

Title B - p. 4 taped
2/15

Sharks

by **Trudi Strain Trueit**

Reading Consultant: Nanci R. Vargus, Ed.D.

 **Marshall Cavendish**
Benchmark
New York

Picture Words

  eyes

 fin

 gills

 mouth

 nose

 shark

 sharks

 tail

 teeth

 can be big!

This has a big .

This 🦈 has
big 👀.

This has a big .

This has big .

This has big .

This has a big .

This has
a big .

Have you ever seen
a big ?

Words to Know

fin (FIN)
> a flap on a fish's body that helps it swim

gills (GILLS)
> the parts of a fish that help it breathe underwater

shark (SHARK)
> a large ocean fish that eats other fish

Find Out More

Books

Markle, Sandra. *Sharks: Biggest! Littlest!* Honesdale, PA:
Boyds Mills Press, 2008.

Pearle, Norman. *Sharks: Ocean Hunters*. New York:
PowerKids Press, 2009.

Sexton, Colleen. *Sharks*. Minneapolis, MN: Bellwether
Media, 2008.

DVDs

Creatures of the Deep: Tiger Shark, Predator Revealed,
National Geographic, 2008.

Planet Carnivore: Sharks and Lions, National Geographic,
2007.

Websites

Monterey Bay Aquarium
www.montereybayaquarium.org/animals/default.aspx
The Shark Research Institute
www.sharks.org/education_kids.htm
Shark Savers
www.sharksavers.org

About the Author

Trudi Strain Trueit lives in Everett, WA, near Puget Sound, and has always been fascinated by sharks, dolphins, and whales. Trudi is the author of more than sixty fiction and nonfiction books for children, including *Starfish* and *Jellyfish* in the Benchmark Rebus Ocean Life series. She writes fiction, too, including the popular *Secrets of a Lab Rat* series. Visit her website at **www.truditrueit.com**.

About the Reading Consultant

Nanci R. Vargus, Ed.D., wants all children to enjoy reading. She used to teach first grade. Now she works at the University of Indianapolis. Nanci helps young people become teachers. She loves to swim in the ocean, but not if there are sharks around. She would rather see sharks from a boat or in an aquarium.

Copyright © 2011 Marshall Cavendish Corporation

Published by Marshall Cavendish Benchmark
An imprint of Marshall Cavendish Corporation

Website: www.marshallcavendish.us

This publication represents the opinions and views of the author based on Trudi Strain Trueit's personal experience, knowledge, and research. The information in this book serves as a general guide only. The author and publisher have used their best efforts in preparing this book and disclaim liability rising directly and indirectly from the use and application of this book.

Other Marshall Cavendish Offices:
Marshall Cavendish International (Asia) Private Limited, 1 New Industrial Road, Singapore 536196 • Marshall Cavendish International (Thailand) Co Ltd. 253 Asoke, 12th Flr, Sukhumvit 21 Road, Klongtoey Nua, Wattana, Bangkok 10110, Thailand • Marshall Cavendish (Malaysia) Sdn Bhd, Times Subang, Lot 46, Subang Hi-Tech Industrial Park, Batu Tiga, 40000 Shah Alam, Selangor Darul Ehsan, Malaysia

Marshall Cavendish is a trademark of Times Publishing Limited

All websites were available and accurate when this book was sent to press.

Library of Congress Cataloging-in-Publication Data
Trueit, Trudi Strain.
Sharks / Trudi Strain Trueit.
    p. cm. — (Ocean life)
Includes bibliographical references.
Summary: "A simple introduction to sharks using rebuses"—Provided by publisher.
ISBN 978-0-7614-4896-9
1. Sharks—Juvenile literature. I. Marshall Cavendish Benchmark. II. Title.
QL638.9.T78 2009
597.3—dc22
2009025474

Editor: Christina Gardeski
Publisher: Michelle Bisson
Art Director: Anahid Hamparian
Series Designer: Virginia Pope

Photo research by Connie Gardner
Cover photo by Paul Souders/*Corbis*

The photographs in this book are used by permission and through the courtesy of: *Getty Images*: p. 2 Jeff Toman, eyes; Jim Cummins, fin; Romilly Lockyer, mouth; David Fletham, nose; p. 3 Brandon Cole, tail; Benne Ochs, teeth; p. 5 Stephen Frink; p. 7 Paul Sutherland; p. 15 Brandon Cole; p. 17 Sami Sarkis; p. 19 Brian Skerry. *Corbis*: p. 9 Jeffrey L. Rotman. *Peter Arnold*: p. 11 Pascal Kobeh; p. 21 J-L Klein and Hubert M.L. *Minden Pictures*: p. 3 Fred Bravendom, shark, sharks; p. 13 Mike Parry. *SuperStock*: p.2 age fotostock, gills.

Printed in Malaysia (T)
1 3 5 6 4 2